Chapter 1

Babies, Children and Transgender

This is undoubtedly going to make more than a few people mad, but once again, I really don't care. I have a voice and a right to use that voice just as you do, and I am fully aware I have already said that in the preface, but until you understand and accept the fact I have those rights without trying to take them away, I will continue to remind you.

Children are the only true innocent souls on this planet, and it is our moral obligation and responsibility to make sure that each one is taken care of, including during the 9 months of pregnancy. If, for some reason, that bothers you, you are a person without compassion or a soul. It absolutely disgusts me to hear some of the vile, ignorant rhetoric that falls out of peoples mouths when it comes to abortion.

In New York, a bill was passed that allows a mother who carried her baby the full 9 months and has gone into labor to decide at that point if she wants the baby or not, if she decides she doesn't the doctors will perform an abortion while she is in labor. California is trying to pass a bill that will give the new mother up to 30 days after delivery to decide if she wants to keep the infant or not, if she decides within those 30 days she doesn't want the baby, she cannot even be questioned or charged by police, even if she commits infanticide. People all over the US cheered and applauded those bills because they protect a woman's right to decide they claimed, what about the rights of the infant??

Let me put this simply so you can understand, IF YOU DON'T WANT TO HAVE A BABY OR ARENT READY OR ARE TOO YOUNG TO HAVE A CHILD, USE BIRTH CONTROL-they make these things called condoms that work quite well at preventing pregnancy. If you aren't responsible enough to be responsible, they maybe you shouldn't be having sex. Abortion is not birth control, I totally understand that accidents happen, women do get raped, those situations are circumstances beyond control and should be taken into consideration and allowed. Getting drunk and taking some guy home and having unprotected sex is your fault, no one else's just yours and if you can't handle your booze don't drink or go to a clinic and have an IUD implant or get on birth control. Why not make birth control easier to get or make it mandatory when your daughter reaches puberty?

Or better yet, how about becoming more active in your child's life, teaching them about the world, themselves and relationships, being a parent instead of an observer. Stop handing your kid everything on a silver platter, you are teaching them they don't have to work to get what they want, you are telling them it's ok to do and be nothing. No one really appreciates anything given to them, they don't pay for it, so they don't respect it. The pride you feel when you want something so bad, you have to work for a long time to get it, and when you finally are able to pay for it yourself, that is a proud moment.

        Understanding that hard work is the key to success is one of life's most important lessons that wasn't taught to the younger generation for quite a long time Taking care of our children means keeping them safe, giving them the education to make them smart, loving them enough to let them be kids, not this craziness they are subjecting our kids to in school. They are teaching kindergarten kindergarten-aged kids in school about sex in the state of Washington.

.Comprehensive sex education in kindergarten through senior year, California encourages their kindergartner teachers to talk about gender identity in class. Wisconsin, for the first time in its history, has made it mandatory to teach sex ed with lessons on transgen derism in kindergarten through 12th grade. NY is pushing for k-12 sex There requirements. There are more states and cities implanting sex ed k-12, , uy question is why?? Children have only one duty as children; to have fun growing up, not learning about sex and gender identity. LET THEM BE KIDS!! My brother played with my Barbie's. I played with his trucks truck, did that mean either of us were the wrong sex in the wrong body? Did I secretly want to be a boy because I played with his trucks? I get that there are some kids who do feel that way, why do we always go the complete extreme opposite because we think that will fix the problem when, in fact, all it does is make the issue insanely worse. Throughout all this, Trans movement not once have I heard one person say "hey how about better counseling in schools that are more student friendly, people who can relate to problems students may be having. Kids need a place or person they can open up and talk to without fear of being judged or ridiculed. How about making punishment for bullies a little harsher to deter them from bullying someone, holding them accountable instead of making excuses?

Stop handing out participation trophies, besides being one of the dumbest policies schools. It doesn't help your child. You are killing the drive within him to be a better person. He doesn't have to try to do anything, because even if he fails to cross the finish line, he still gets rewarded for failing. You are teaching them that being a loser is ok OK. What happened to wanting better for our kids?

There is a fine line between discipline and abuse, but a child has to be taught right from wrong as well as there are consequences for every action we do. Placating them is like putting a dirty band-aid on an open wound. Eventually that wound is going to fester before turning into a bad infection from the dirty band-aid. Taking away the parents' ability and right to discipline their child hasn't stopped child abuse children. In fact, child abuse cases have only gotten worse, more extreme in how they abuse their children. In 2021, sadly, the first year child abuse statistics started to be kept, 1,820 children died due to abuse, with parents making up 77% of the offenders of neglect is the most common abuse. The Child Advocacy Center investigated 247,543 cases in 2022 involving claims of sexual abuse. That number is 58% of the total abuse cases they investigated that year alone.

      The FXB Center for Health and Human Rights at Harvard University and the International Organization for Migration conducted research on child trafficking, publishing a report in 2023. They analyzed 20 years of data gathered from over 69,000 victims across 186 countries from the IOM data bases. They found that globally, 50% of the victims are recruited by friends or family, increased vulnerability to trafficking where they had little or no education or lived in low income or poverty level homes. Methods of control included false promises, psychological and physical abuse as well as threats. 43% of the victims, mainly boys, were trafficked for forced labor in industries like domestic work, begging and agriculture, 21% mostly girls but with the number of boys rising quickly, were forced into prostitution, pornography and sexual servitude. A report in 2021 from the United Nations stated that the number of children trafficked has tripled, while the number of boys taken has increased by 5x in the last 15 years. Child/human trafficking is the largest crime network the world has ever seen, it has already surpassed illegal arms trade and drugs in revenue.

No doubt that what I am about to say is going to make a lot of people angry, but it needs to be said. I am not homophobic or transphobic, your life choices are your own but when those choices begin to effect children, then I have a problem. Madeline Kirksey, manager of Children's Lighthouse Learning Center and a co worker, Akesha Wyatt, were both fired for refusing to accept a 6 year old boy as a girl who was being transgendered by his same sex parents. What the hell is wrong with people, do they honestly believe that a 6 year old child that probably just learned to tie his shoes, defiantly doesn't understand penis's and vagina's, doesn't even know how babies are born and probably can't even write or spell his own name but yet has the mental knowledge to decide he wants to transgender! Does that make any sense to you? What about the couple where the man transgendered to a woman, the woman to a man, decided to have a baby so the woman who is a man (not fully Trans) got pregnant, gave birth at home and the man who is now a woman was breast feeding the baby while she talked about having to bottle feed the baby because she/he wasn't producing any milk. So why would they let the baby suck on his nipple, no nutritional value is being achieved, no milk at all so it's just a baby sucking on a man's nipple, which sounds a lot like sexual abuse of a child.

We have no business transgender ing children. I don't believe that anyone really knows what they want until they reach adulthood and have lived life a little. If we are completely honest with ourselves, we would admit that the things we thought we were so important growing up turned out to be not so important, the things we wanted so badly when we were young weren't things we wanted when we grew up. Children don't have the mental capacity or knowledge to make such life-altering decisions and parents shouldn't have the power to make those decisions for them, not when it is a decision that is an extreme change in life like transgender ing. Basically, what I am trying to say and failing miserably at it is let kids be kids, let them decide for themselves when they get older if they want to transition to the opposite sex. Have them talk to a therapist for a period of no less than a year to determine if it is really want they want or not, do whatever needs to be done to help your child make the best informed decision he can make without any pressure from wanted parents, peers or society. Puberty is hard enough without this added extra insanity, stop sexualizing kids. I am not against anyone transgender ing as long as they are at an age where they know without a doubt that is what they want to do, not just because every other kid in school is doing it or society tells them to. A parent posted on Tik Tok about their son's kindergarten teacher dressing his son up in a dress and telling him he was really a girl trapped in a boy's body. The boy was extremely distraught over what his teacher did because he had told his teacher over and over again no, he didn't want to put on the dress but was forced to anyway. Teachers are supposed to teach children how to write, do math, read, not tell them they are the wrong sex. That kind of education is not education, it is brainwashing. Children are so impressionable and when you have teachers like that, what do you think is going to be the outcome?

So far, children have to face abuse, extreme abortions, transgender ing, child trafficking, but this next issue is one that has only come to light within the last 10 years or so and that is drag queens and transgender's wearing provocative clothing, at times daisy duke shorts exposing part of their genitalia, gyrating and dancing sexually for children.

HTTP://www.youtube.com/watch?v=efp9X3xtbyc

HTTP://www.youtube.com/watch?v=jkZujRnHWNA

HTTP://www.dailymail.co.uk/news/article-11317925/Shocking-footage-family-friendly-drag-queen-sees-performer-spreading-legs-kids.html

HTTP://www.youtube.com/watch?v=ZmQVNTAq050

HTTP://www.dailymail.co.uk/video/video/video-1371067/Sexy-dancers-twerk-young-boys-children-s-party.html

https://nypost.com/2023/03/29/girl-straddled-by-drag-queen-at-North-Carolina-school-sparking-outrage/

I think that any drag queen or Trans. ANYONE who participates in basically a table dance for a child could possibly have pedophile tendencies, and once again, before you label me transphobic, answer me this question-what adult would dance in a sexual manner for a child in the first place? Someone who doesn't have an attraction to children wouldn't think that would be an acceptable thing to do. It has nothing to do with Transgender. It's about someone performing like that for a child and the Trans Movement has placed Trans people in the spotlight. And if you can honestly tell me after watching the videos I provided above, that they are not sexual in nature and the sexual nature of their dance directed at those children isn't wrong, you are either blind, ignorant or both

.   The fact that we even have to talk about sex with young children is an indicator of how depraved society has become. In Russia, President Putin just passed a law making it a crime to talk to anyone under the age of 18 about the LGBTQ Transmat Movement, punishable by up to two years in prison. I agree with him 100% because this isn't about society accepting gay, lesbian or trans people, it stopped being about that in New York, when they kicked off Pride month with its annual Drag March where hundreds of drag performers and trans people shouted "WE'RE HERE WE'RE QUEER WE ARE COMING FOR YOUR CHILDREN!"

        Gays Against Groomers is an organization campaigning against gender-affirming care for minors, as well as school curriculum content that has LGBTQ themes, as well as criticizing Drag Queen Story Hour. This is what their website says:

"   Gays Against Groomers is a 501(c)4 nonprofit organization of gay people and others within the community who oppose the recent trend of indoctrinating, sexualizing and medicalizing children under the guise of "LGBTQIA+"

It also says:

Our community that once preached love and acceptance of others has been hijacked by radical activists who are now pushing extreme concepts into society, specifically targeting children in recent years.

The overwhelming majority of gay people are against what the community has transformed into, and we do not accept the political movement pushing their agenda in our name. Gays Against Groomers directly opposes the sexualization and indoctrination of children. This includes drag queen story hours, drag shows involving children, the transitioning and medicalization of minors, and gender theory being taught in the classroom.

The activists, backed by school boards, the government, the woke media, and corporations, have been speaking on our behalf for too long. When fighting for equality, our goal was to successfully integrate ourselves into society, but now these radicals aim to restructure it entirely in order to accommodate a fringe minority, as well as seek to indoctrinate children into their ideology. We're saying NO."

I applaud their courage to speak out and make it clear where they stand. The rabbit hole can get very dark once you start down it and knowing there are organizations like Gays Against Grooming makes the journey a little easier. Grooming is the normalization of inappropriate behavior or an abnormal relationship with the end goal being sexual abuse. Manipulation and brainwashing are the tools used to twist the abnormal in normal life. The groomers engage in sexual, physical and emotional abuse, sometimes forcing the child to do violent or illegal acts,

These are seven signs to watch for as they could indicate your child may be being groomed:

1.the person is taking a quick, significant interest in you and your life, like giving gifts for no reason

2. They tell you to keep secrets, like "don't tell your mom, but I think she is too hard on you."

3. Discussing inappropriate adult subjects with you such as intimate relationships or sex.

4. They try to fulfill your needs, like making themselves readily available to listen to you and make you feel safe, that you can confide in them. They want you to rely on them.

5. They start trying to spend time alone with you, they will try to make it seem as innocent as they can.

6. They give you drugs or alcohol, which is one of the most dangerous tools they use, because mind-altering substances can lower a person's inhibitions or their ability to even recall the abuse the next day. GHB is also known as a date rape drug. It is odorless, colorless, tasteless and can be put in drinks or food. It causes blackouts, but the body still functions somewhat.

7. They touch you inappropriately in inappropriate areas.
Finally, I couldn't end this without addressing this article that appeared on "COLLEGE FIX." which is supported by the "Student Free Press Association."
On May 17, 2019-they reported that Pascal Gagneux, a professor at the University of San Diego-called unborn children "legitimate Parasites" during an in class slide show. Even though this caused major backlash and criticism from people all over, the university defended his statement, claiming that it is a widely accepted scientific concept. Michael Behuke, an assistant professor of pathobiological sciences, (meaning he

studies parasites) said the Geneagenesis remark "wasn't just bad science, it was borderline satanic."

Lastly, NAMBLA is an active web site. NAMBLA stands for "NATIONAL MAN/BOY LOVERS ASSOCIATION." They are a pedophilia and pederasty advocacy organization headquartered in the United States,, working to abolish age of consent laws that criminalize adult sexual involvement with minors doesn't hide what they are all about, but my question is why is that website even allowed to be online? Why hasn't the FBI or our government down an investigation there because obviously there is sexual abuse happening there?

This is copied directly from the main page of their website:

"NAMBLA's goal is to end the extreme oppression of men and boys in mutually consensual relationships by:

1,) building understanding and support for such relationships;
2.) educating the general public on the benevolent nature of man/boy love;
cooperating with lesbian, gay, feminist, and other liberation movements;
supporting the liberation of persons of all ages from sexual prejudice and oppression.
3.) Participation, only in the above context, is open to everyone sympathetic to man/boy love and personal freedom. We cannot facilitate contacts bewtween

individuals other than for the above enumerated purposes.

NAMBLA calls for the empowerment of youth in all areas, not just the sexual. We support greater economic, political and social opportunities for young people and denounce the rampant ageism that segregates and isolates them in fear and mistrust. We believe sexual feelings are a positive life force. We support the rights of youth as well as adults to choose the partners with whom they wish to share and enjoy their bodies.

We condemn sexual abuse and all forms of coercion. Freely-chosen relationships differ from unwanted sex. Present laws, which focus only on the age of the participants, ignore the quality of their relationships. We know that differences in age do not preclude mutual, loving interaction between persons. NAMBLA is strongly opposed to age-of-consent laws and all other restrictions which deny men and boys the full enjoyment of their bodies and control over their own lives.

We call for fundamental reform of the laws regarding relations between youths and adults. Today, many thousands of men and boys are unjustly ground into the disfunctional criminal justice system. Blindly, this system condemns consensual, loving relationships between younger and older people. NAMBLA's Prisoner Program, with limited resources, works to provide a modicum of humanity to some of these people. Click here to find out more.

NAMBLA is a political, civil rights, and educational organization. We provide factual information and help educate society about the positive and beneficial nature of man/boy love."

There isn't any doubt that every member of that site is a pedophile, this isn't found on the dark web, this is the link to their site.
https://www.nambla.org/welcome.html
Why is this site even still up? The following email I copied directly from their "Why NAMBLA Matters" section:

For over 40 years, NAMBLA has been the primary voice testifying to the benevolent aspects of man/boy love.
NAMBLA has been, and continues to be, a beacon of moral support for all individuals who feel a natural love for boys.
Through our web site and publications, NAMBLA provides a public forum for a diverse range of viewpoints supporting sexual liberation and youth liberation.
NAMBLA is the only organization that specifically supports incarcerated individuals who identify as boy lovers or who otherwise agree with our aims.
NAMBLA has celebrated the dignity inherent in the natural love of boys.
NAMBLA has been a bulwark against the lies and pejoratives of a venal abuse industry and opportunistic politicians and law enforcement officials.

Exposing these lies is important not only for man/boy lovers but for all people who value democracy, since its foundation is a well-informed electorate.

NAMBLA has consistently protested ill advised wars that needlessly maim and kill young people and devastate families here and abroad. Even before it started, NAMBLA warned against the Iraq invasion. Our warning was on our Web site long before many of the politicians, who belatedly recognized their immense error, echoed our concerns.

NAMBLA has spoken out strongly against the shoddy and disrespectful treatment afforded youth in our society and the resulting high rates of child and youth poverty, neglect and alienation.

NAMBLA has consistently highlighted injustices and harm in age of consent laws. Instead of protecting young people, these laws have done the very opposite."

All this and more isn't on the Dark Web, it is on regular internet where anyone, including young, confused boys can go to meet a pedophile. There are letters in fact from boys as young as 12 years old, writing about the "love" they share with these older disgusting pedophiles.

There is so much perversion, open pedophilla on this site it is disgusting, once again i ask, why is it still online? VirPed (virtuous pedophile) that claims to be a site meant to help pedophiles from acting out their desires, salt peter or castration I think would work the best. In today's woke culture, it is now politically incorrect to call a pedophile a pedophile, we are now supposed to call them "MAP'S" or minor attracted person's. Sorry, but I choose to be politically incorrect on this one.

The fact those two sites exist on the internet, (not the dark web) shows just how far down a very dark hole this world has fallen.

Protecting children starts with knowing what evils you are facing, educating yourself so you are aware of the tactics evil uses and speaking out without fear against those evils. Children don't have a voice unless you speak for them.

Matthew 18:6

"It would be better for him if a millstone were hung around his neck and he were cast into the sea than that he should cause one of these little ones to sin."

Chapter 2

Things Are Not Always What They Seem

"I do solemnly swear (or affirm) that I will faithfully execute the Office of President of the United States, and will to the best of my Ability, preserve, protect and defend the Constitution of the United States."

Administered and worded in accordance with Article II Section 1 of the US Constitution, the presidential oath is written in the Constitution, for

federal officials and congress, the Constitution only
states "they be bound by Affirmation or by Oath to
support this constitution." This oath was established
by Abraham Lincoln in April 1961 during the civil war,
loyalties at that time were prone to switch sides, this
oath is an affirmation of loyalty to the Constitution, not
a government or party.

In April 1961, Abraham Lincoln, enacted a bill
requiring both Senate and congress to also be sworn in
with an oath, he feared the loyalties of his fellow
politicians could not be trusted due to the civil war .
The civil war pit brother against brother, ripped the
country in two, so President Lincoln added the oath to
ensure that whoever was elected were loyal to this
nati9on and it's consti9tution.

It isn't our constitution that is corrupt,
oppressive or racist, it is those who are in power,
abusing that power for their own personal gain, those
who we have unfortunately elected into office that are
deceitful and corrupt. People who, when elected, aren't
multi millionaires and the salary they make while being
either Senator or congress person is on average around
150000 dollars per year. Follow the money and you'll
find the corruption, big pharma and oil companies give
kick backs to politicians who put the interests of
whoever is paying the most money.

But corruption is more than money, it's
dishonesty, lies and manipulation. It is a lie so deep
and complex, so well thought out and perpetrated that
the liar believes his own lies. It is an absence of truth,

honor, and most importantly, loyalty to this country, it's citizens and our Constitution.

How have they managed to do this without us knowing, how did become so blind? Why is it almost impossible for people to accept or believe the truth while embracing every single lie? Easy, its called propaganda.

Propaganda is information that is biased, misleading or a lie that is used to promote or publicize a political cause or view. It is primarily used to influence or persuade by dissemination of information (ie facts, arguments, rumors, half truths or lies, often conveyed through mass media.) It is a systematic effort to manipulate other peoples beliefs, attitudes or actions. Propagandists have a specific goal or set of goals, to achieve this, they deliberately choose what facts or arguments they need and present them in the way they believe will have the best effect. To maximize the effect, they omit or distort pertinent facts into lies or just simply lie. The also try to divert the attention of the people from the truth so the only thing they see is the propaganda they are being told.

Psychological warfare is another form of propaganda but differs in the fact it is used in pre war or war time to confuse or demoralize enemy populations or troops, keeping them unaware and off guard in the face of coming attacks or inducing them to surrender. Political warfare encompasses propaganda along with other techniques during peacetime to intensify social and political division, creating confusion and tension within the societies of targeted states.

Brainwashing is another concept relating to propaganda, usually meaning an intensive political indoctrination. The methods used to brainwash and individual or group is solitary confinement, threats, humiliation in front of peers (social media shaming) Media is the vehicle used to deliver propaganda in all these different forms to the public.

Signs, symbols even words can be used as propaganda to influence populations minds, almost anything can be used as propaganda. The responsibility lies within every person to use what is between their ears, that thing that God gave each of us- our brain. Propaganda only succeeds when the population blindly believes. Knowledge is power, the more you learn, the more time you take to educate yourself the less likely you are to believe the lies.

Don't just accept whatever video you see, article you read, news you hear as fact. Look at the author, who wrote or posted it, do some research and find out who they are, where they went to school, who they worked for and who they work for now, what their religious beliefs are, what their political affiliation is. This information will give you tell you what you need to discern the validity of what they are trying to get you to believe, what their hidden agenda is. And keep in mind that just because 10 people tell you the same story does not make it true, it could just be that those 10 people heard the same story or are working together to make you believe their lie.

Because Fox News runs a story does not make it a lie, you need to be smarter than those trying to dumb you down.

We are silent on the issues that matter but lose our minds over problems that are non existent, exaggerated or don't really matter. We have forgotten how to think for ourselves because we have our noses buried in our cell phones all day, We are so lost in social media we don't know how to be social around people. We choose to accept the lies rather than the responsibility of the truth. Even the definitions of words have been changed to fit their narrative or agenda (narcissist which once was defined as someone who loves themselves and thinks they are better than anyone else is now used as a blanket label for everything from abuse to depression, nationalist which once meant a person who loves their country and thinks it's better than any other country is now defined as being a Nazi)

Joe Biden has betrayed this country, the constitution and every citizen of the United States. He has broken the oath he pledged on January 6, 2020 by allowing open borders, not caring about American citizens and inflation, sending billions to Ukraine while ignoring the fact that most Americans cant afford to even buy groceries. His hatred for America grows more apparent every day with his complete lack of concern for the security of the US. He, I believe, has committed crimes against this country that are treasonous at the very least.

His son, Hunter Biden, has somehow managed to avoid any prosecution over his laptop that was turned in by a computer repair store owner. Little has been heard from main stream media or the democrats concerning the pictures that were found on the hard drive but 51 former intelligence officers signed a public letter during the 2020 presidential campaign claiming that the contents of the laptop-full of pictures of Hunter with prostitutes, drug usage by Hunter and pictures of foreign business deals-was a Russian campaign to influence the election.

Just one of the over 10000 pictures found on Hunter's hard drive which all can be seen at https://bidenlaptopmedia.com/. There is no doubt after

visiting the site that it is Hunter's hard drive, not a Russian campaign to influence the election, no one forced him to do drugs or film himself having sex with prostitutes. Hunter Biden was visiting the white house during the time they found cocaine in the oval office, must be a Russian campaign right?

(When are American citizens going to realize that any time one of the Democrats are caught red handed doing something they shouldn't, they immediately blame Russia?)

One official, only known as "Whistle blower X", is a 13 year IRS employee and special agent with IRS Criminal Investigation who was in charge of the agency's investigation into Hunter's tax crimes spanning 5 years claimed his bosses and the Department of Justice "obstructed" his investigation and was told to ignore any evidence that implicated the President.

The following WhatsApp messages show that on July 30, 2017 Hunter sent his partner at CEFC, a Chinese oil giant, a message revealing Joe's involvement and knowledge of his son's business dealings.

This is just one example of the family corruption in the Biden family, yet main stream media and the Democrats would have you believing that this is all a lie, an elaborate plan enacted by the Russians to influence the presidential campaign. The pictures leave no room for doubt that they are Hunter Biden, the screen shots found on the laptop taken by Hunter of Whatsapp messages also implicate "the big guy" in Hunter's business dealings. The evidence is there but without the help of the American people standing behind the few senators and congressmen trying to bring these crimes to light, nothing will ever happen. They are succeeding in their deception.

We have been lied to about so many things, including being made to believe the truth was a lie. Don't fall into that trap of thinking our history, what we were taught in school is a lie, the only lie is telling us it was a lie. Everything they do has an ulterior motive, an end goal they want to achieve, there isn't anything or anyone they will not hesitate to sacrifice to attain what they want. This is not only an attack on who we as American's are but where we come from and very fabric of who we are.

There is a growing number of people who believe that Joe Biden is only a puppet who is being controlled by someone else. Obama appeared on "Late Night With Stephen Colbert" in the beginning of November 2020. Colbert asked Obama "Did you ever look at something on the news and say, You know what this situation need? A little Barrack Obama?" Obama laughed, his answer was about a "third term" and a "stand in."

"OBAMA: I said this before. People would ask me, "Knowing what you know now, do you wish you had a third term?" And I used to say, "You know what? If I could make an arrangement where I had a stand-in, a front man or front woman, and they had an earpiece in and I was just in my basement in my sweats looking through the stuff, and then I could sort of deliver the lines, but somebody else was doing all the talking and ceremony, I'd be fine with that. Because I found the work fascinating. I mean, I write about the... even on my worst days, I found puzzling out, you know, these big, complicated, difficult issues, especially if you were working with some great people, to be professionally really satisfying. But I do not miss having to wear a tie every day."

Ironically enough, Biden seems to prove every time he appears in public to not be mentally competent by rambling while giving a speech to appearing to have handlers while out in public. Obama and Hillary Clinton have been seen at almost every important gathering or party, not too far from Joe's side, almost as if they are monitoring his actions and words. Conspiracy theory, absolutely, but every conspiracy theory has some truth in it.

Obama stated in a pod cast in 2015 with Mark Maron

"The legacy of slavery, Jim Crow, discrimination in almost every institution of our lives. You know, that casts a long shadow and that's still part of our DNA that's passed on. We're not cured of it. Racism we are not cured of, clearly."

Americans are racist the day they are born, according to Obama, it's in our genetic makeup. That statement is racist itself, but his racism and hatred for America is apparent, no matter how much he tries to hide it. His contempt for America shows in verified pictures of him standing with his hands clasped together in front of him instead of his hand over his heart while the National Anthem played when he was senator, but during his presidency in May 2009 at Arlington's National Cemetery's memorial Amphitheater in conjunction with a Memorial Day wreath laying ceremony at the Tomb of the Unknown Soldier, once again he stood with his hands clasped in front of him.

Michelle Obama said "Americans weren't ready for her natural hair" so she kept her hair straightened because Americans hadn't adjusted to a black first family. She kept it that way out of fear her hair would be used as a distraction or politicized, keeping it straight would allow the administration to focus on their agenda instead of having to answer racist questions about her hair. Are we that small minded and stupid that all the American people were concerned about was her hair?

She also said during a speech that she woke up everyday in a house built by black slaves, and to a certain degree, she is right. Historians have found around 300 slaves helped to build the White House, slavery is wrong on any level. But you cannot judge the past by today, life was completely different 200 years ago and slavery was unfortunately a part of every day life. You cannot pick and choose who you hold responsible for slavery, every single nationality and race has been slaves at some point, but let's be honest here. The first man in the US to own a slave was a black man, there were over 3500 black slaves owners as well, being a slave owner was not restricted to only white people. Slavery has never been inclusive to whites or a white only crime, if you hold one accountable, you must hold all accountable

You cannot judge the past by today's standards, how things are viewed today are different than even 5 years ago so you have to look at the entire picture before deciding if the painter was good or not. Every civilization at some point or another has had slaves, even today slavery is still a part of some places. Holding one race responsible while ignoring the truth doesn't do anything except make you the actual racist in this situation.

Arrack and Michelle acted as if they were the victims of racism perpetuated towards them by the same people who put them in the White House. Barrack's precipice against whites is more than apparent in his book "The Audacity of Hope." In it he laments:

"I can't help but view the American experience through the lens of a black man of mixed heritage, forever mindful of how generations of people who looked like me were subjugated and stigmatized, and the subtle and not so subtle ways that race and class continue to shape our lives."

"Conservatives for instance, tend to bristle when it comes to government interference in the marketplace or their right to bear
arms. Yet many of these same conservatives show little to no concern when it comes to government wiretapping without a warrant or government attempts to control people's sexual practices."

Obama voted for a law that expanded the government's ability to eavesdrop on cellular communications inside the US on American citizens without a warrant. It provided immunity to phone companies who participated in NSA wiretapping programs. He also signed a one year extension of several controversial elements of the Patriot Act, which allows the government to petition the Foreign Intelligence Surveillance Court to "compel" businesses to hand over customer records. It also includes Section 215 which allows the use of roving wiretaps and the so called "lone wolf" provision. (allows surveillance of individuals with no known ties to any terrorist organization)

During Obama's administration, the NSA required Verizon to hand over ALL of its metadata for ALL of the calls made on the Verizon network. The following are just some of what someone can learn from the metadata on your cell phone:

1. Location and time a user accessed certain online accounts.
2. Phone call duration, call status (incoming, outgoing, or canceled), date and time, call type (voice or video).
3. Software application install and uninstall dates for, their use frequency, and even usage time.
4. Camera or device used to take a photo, whether was a downloaded photo or not, capture date, time, and GPS location, deletion status.
5. Device or browser used to send an email, its delivery time, or even show an email was spoofed.
6. What time of day or night did you usually communicate? By text or phone call?
5. Were there group chats? Who else was involved?
7. How often did you talk or text?
8. Who usually initiated communication?
9. Was communication mutually reciprocated?

So much for his claim of being against government spying on it's citizens. There is so much about Obama that doesn't add up or make sense, but because this country was so caught up in electing the first black President along with the fear of being labeled a racist, we didn't ask any questions, we just looked the other way.

With today's technology, you can find out anything about anyone if you look hard and deep enough, especially school records and transcripts. If you attended Washington State University in 1995, there is a record of that, there is a record of your school transcripts as well. The process to get a copy of your transcripts is as follows:

1. Contact your college's office of the registrar or admissions, or use a third-party verification agency if your college uses one.
2. Choose how you will request your transcripts: online, by mail, by phone, by fax, or in person.
3. Fill out a transcript request form and pay a small fee if required.
4. Provide proof of identification and written consent if needed.
5. Wait for your transcripts to be sent to you or to the institution of your choice.

Not a very hard process by any means, seems very easy to me since if a person applies for another college or perhaps a job that requires certain qualifications that need to be verified before hiring would need to see a copy of those transcripts. There is more to this mystery but before I go any further, you need to understand something about the Internet and Google.

Google is an American search engine company, founded in 1998 by Sergey Brin and Larry Page. More than 70% of worldwide online search requests are handled by Google, (think about how many times a day or even a week you search something on your PC or phone and then multiply that by billions) Google purchased youtube in 2006 for 1.65 billion in stocks, but did not merge the two companies, choosing to run it as a separate entity. Google released Chrome in 2008 and passed Microsoft's Internet Explorer in 2012 and to date, is the number one browser. In 2005, Google acquired Android Inc, but at that time, Android had not released any products. Two years later, Google announced the founding of the Open Handset Alliance, a consortium of dozens of technology and mobile telephone companies, including Intel Corporation, Motorola, Inc., NVIDIA Corporation, Texas Instruments Incorporated, LG Electronics, Inc., Samsung Electronics, Sprint Nextel Corporation, and T-Mobile (Deutsche Telekom). The consortium was created in order to develop and promote Android, a free open-source operating system based on Linux. By the end of 2011, Android had a 52% global market share, surpassing even Apple. In August 2015, Google was reorganized into a subsidiary of the holding company Alphabet Inc. but Alphabet again reorganized in 2017 to create an intermediate holding company, XXVI Holdings, and to convert Google into a limited liability company (LLC).

Sergey Brin and Larry Page have been accused of being liberal, which they have denied but ironically, in the 2020 election year, 88% of Google employees donated to the Democratic party. So keep in mind while Googling for something, the results you may find could possibly be biased or left leaning and one sided.

Even with "Russian Hackers" that the left loves to blame everything on, no one has been able to locate any transcripts of Obama's time at Columbia University. Even his class mates have no memory of him whatsoever, which is strange because if you went to school with someone who later became President of the United States, you would remember at least if you shared a class or sat next to him. The only "proof" is a picture of someone he claims was his room mate and a radical professor's stating he attended Columbia.

I am not saying he is a fraud, I do believe that myself but what you choose to believe is completely up to you. I just hope you take the time to do your own research and draw your own conclusion. There is so much more to what is going on than what main stream media tells us. We are only told what they feel is necessary or if it fits into their agenda. It is up to each and every one of us to do what it takes to find out what the truth is, but even that isn't enough.

The only way anything is ever going to change is when we put aside our differences and come together, demand that wrongs be made right and stop letting the fear of being labeled something we know we aren't keep us from speaking out and standing up for what and who we believe in. Until then, we are doomed to continue down this path of destruction they are leading us on.

Chapter 3

Propaganda and Palestine

We have been blind to what has been happening right before our eyes but is it too late? Perhaps, if you choose to give up easily without a fight but this country and the principals it was founded upon are worth fighting for, freedom is worth fighting for.

There are many ways to wage war on a country without the use of armies, guns or bombs. Often times the most effective weapon isn't one that will kill you but instead change the very fabric of who you are. People tend to forget that those in power own or control main stream media, they donate or finance morning news shows, television shows, almost every outlet that people recieve information from is what those in power want you to know, nothing more.

Dumbing down the population is a form of control that is also used by those in power to control and manipulate the population. There has been a huge movement in the last few years to change our history, almost everything we have been taught for years in school has been taken out of textbooks or just isn't part of the core curriculum anymore. How is a person living today more knowledgeable of our history than the historians who lived through our history? I don't buy into the claims that we have been lied to about our history, I refuse to accept that lie-and yes, it is a complete lie.

It doesn't take a rocket scientist to figure out why those in power would want us to accept their lies. If we do, if we choose to just roll over and let ourselves be convinced by their illusion of truth, then we are not even a shadow of those who came and fought before us, those who established and defended our freedoms deserve more respect and honor than cowardice and weakness.

      Deception is :
1.) Disinformation is false information deliberately spread to deceive people.
2,)Disinformation is an orchestrated adversarial activity in which actors employ strategic deceptions and media manipulation tactics to advance political, military, or commercial goals.

      Deception is another term for a lie, anything that isn't the truth, even if it is made to appear as truth, is in fact, still deception or a lie. Corrupt politicians, main stream media, journalists, influencers, social media and more can all be a part of if not the perpatrator itself, of deception. Why do they use deception or lies? They are used to achieve the end goal they desire, easier done if you, the public, believes that the goal they are trying to reach is beneficial or a just cause. Manipulating the facts is a way of being able to attain what they desire with the least amount of resistance.

      Psychological warfare is nothing like conventional combat, it does not rely on physical force but instead, attacks the power of the mind through different tactics. Dissemination and spreading of propaganda and misinformation, issuing of threats, all aimed at influincing perception and behaviors. Their fundamental objective is to demoralize the enemy, plant seeds of doubt and in turn, controlling the enemys decision making process without any need for physical attack. It kind of like living in an abusive relationship where the abuser, through beatings and degradation, eventually controls every aspect of his victim's life.

The use of horrific atrocities to demoralize an enemy population has been a tactic used for hundreds of years. The use of rape is believed to not only degrade and demoralize the victim but other family members as well psychologically. Recent examples of such measures are Hutu massacres of minority Tutsi in Burundi in 1994, after the breakup of Yugoslavia in the 1990's and in Isreal on October 7, 2023. The systematic use of mass rape and murder is also used to force the relocation of civilians through fear during an ethnic cleansing campaign as well as cause life long problems for the victims.

The Israel/Gaza war is a prime example of psychological warfare today. Protestors in the United States are calling Hamas "freedom fighters" ignoring the brutal actions committed by Hamas and other Palestinian terrorists on October 7, 2023. They forget or choose to believe the propaganda lies being put out on youtube, twitter, tiktok or telegram such as Israel actually killed it's own citizens. They forget that each and every one of the terrorists wore GoPro cameras that day, so their brutality was captured on film. They were also seen on camera calling their parents in Gaza, bragging about how many Jews they had killed, standing on the head or bodies of victims as well as videos too horrible to be seen.

The Holocaust is one of the worst, if not the worst act of genocide committed against any people ever and children in the Middle East are taught it never happened! In the Middle East, children are taught that the Jews died of disease or starvation and the number of Jews who were killed was exaggerated. They are taught that the gas chambers are just a lie made up by the Jews and the west, the concentration camps were not bad and that Hitler didn't have the Jews murdered.

The Palestinian propaganda machine has been working overtime during the Israel-Gaza war, flooding every media outlet with lies every chance they get, hoping the rest of the world will believe their story. Sadly, the rest of the world is doing just that, as in the case of Shireen Abu Akleh, an Al Jazeera correspondent.

On May 11, 2023 during a Israel Defense Raid in the West Bank, an incursion aimed to apprehend a terrorist operating in the city of Jenin, a hotbed for Hamas and Islamic Jihad activity. it was also "home" to the Palestinians who went on a shooting spree in Bnei Brak before slaughtering 3 innocent civilians in Elad on May 5. In total, there were 5 terrorist attacks the were successfully committed by Palestenians as well as Arab citizens that had migrated to Israel, during the Islamic holy month of Ramadan and in honor of the 74th anniversary of "Nakba" (the Arabic word for the "catastrophe" of Israel's establishment in 1948)

When the IDF entered Jenin, their intention was not to hurt or kill innocent civilians but to eliminate a known terrorist. The Palestinian Authority press, which is controlled by President Mahoud Abbas, claimed that Israeli snipers intentionally targeted Abu Akleh even though she clearly wore a PRESS vest, which of course the IDF and Israel venhemontly denies.

Israel has very strict rules of engagement, so stringent that men and women of the IDF often hesitate to shoot to kill because if they hurt an innocent civilian, they face criminal prosecution and court martial. Their first action after Akleh's death was sincere condolences to the family and opening an investigation.

The purpose for the investigation is to determine if IDF or Palestinian shooters are responsible for her death, either way the Israeli government have been very open and transparant in their desire to identify the origin of the ammunition to determine who is responsible for her death. The Palestinian Authority's agenda isn't about cooperating with Israel so they refused to hand over the bullet for ballistics, they did no testing themselves but instead they went to the International Criminal Court, demanding Israel be censured.

CNN conducted an "investigation" of their own (keep in mind the there were 2 CNN reporters that knew about Oct 7 2023 prior to the attack, and in fact rode into Israel with the terrorists) claiming "new evidence" that the IDF was responsible, but the footage never actually showed Abu Akleh being shot.

"Eye witnesses" of course were on hand, among them were Palestinian journalist Shatha Hanaysha and Professor Jamal; Huwail of the Arab American University in Jenin. Both claimed to of seen the IDF intentionally fire on Abu Akleh, but what CNN failed to inform us of is who those 2 "eye witnesses" were.

Hanaysha champions "Martyrs" (a muslim who dies deliberatly in the name of Allah, the act of sacrificing one's life to bear witness one's faith in Islam and a martyr is given 7 blessings from Allah as well as 72 virgins. A muslim who dies in the battlefield fighting the unbelievers achieves the highest rank of martyrdom) The martyrs Hanaysha champions are those who are killed while attempting and succeeding at slaughtering Jews as she so proudly glorifies her "comrades-in-arms" on her social media without apology.

Huwail, a member of Abba's Fatah faction, once a parliamentarian in the Palestinian Legislative Council and current member of the Fatah Revolutionary Council from Jenin, said in an interview on Lebanon's Al-Mayadeen tv that the terrorist who carried out the attack in Bnei Brak that left 5 Israeli's dead "brought light into the hearts of Palestinians."

Just to clarify what is meant when you hear someone claim that Israel "occupies" the Palestinian lands and are oppressing the Palestinian people so there isn't any confusion-the land they are referring to isn't palestine or gaza or the west bank, they are speaking about Israel. It is the term used to describe the lands captured and occupied by Israel which Palestine consideres illegal.

So, who was there first? That is a topic of many heated debates, but what is the truth?? If we look at history and the Bible, Moses led the Jews to the Promised land which is now Israel in the 13 bc-almost 3000 years prior to the term Palestine or Palestinian even coming to use.

The term "Palestine" does not appear nor is mentioned in the Quran, it does not appear or is mentioned in the new or old testament until the Hebrew concordance of the King James Bible in eight verses. It is still unknown where the word "palestine" originated but is believed to of been from the Egyptian and Hebrew word "pleshet"- meaning rolling or migratory. It was used to describe the people living northeast of Egypt, the Phillistines. They were an Aegean people more closely related to Greeks and actually had no ethnic,linguistic or historical connection or relation to Arabia.

Something else I would like to clarify is this=the Bible has never been rewritten like so many people believe. Rewritten means to edit, start over or make significant changes so no, the Bible hasn't been rewritten. The King James Version is simply the language changed from Hebrew to English, the only thing changed was the language.

Egyptians called what is now Israel, Syria and Lebanon. The name "Israel" was first used in the 10th century bc, referring to the northern Jewish land after the division of King Solomons kingdom.

Archaeologists have discovered dozens of sites they refer to as the "Iron Age," (1200-1000B.c.) proving the existence of Israeli settlements in Canaan and today, scholars have a new theory based on the evidence they have found. That new theory goes against the previous one of believing that Israelites came from the desert fringes to the east either by military conquest or peaceful infiltration. Archaeologists and scholars now believe that the early Israelites were actually indigenous to Canaan and were "pastoralists" (herders and farmers of livestock) living on the edges of settlements. Anson F Rainey wrote "Inside, Outside, Where Did The Early Israelites Come From?" and in it he presents very compelling evidence that the earliest Israelites actually arose in the vest lands east of Jordan, exactly as the Bible states.

So when did Palestinian's first appear in history? Until 1920, there weren't any Arab Palestinian's, until the late 19th century, inhabitants of the area between the Jordan River and Mediterranean Sea referred to themselves primarily by their religion. Prior to 1920, there isn't any mention of "Palestine." "Palestine" is not mentioned in the Quran, new or old testaments but does occur in atleast 8 verses of the Hebrew concordance of the King James Bible.

It is believed that the name "Palestine" is derived from the Egyptian and Hebrew word "peleshet" meaning rolling or migratory. This word was used to describe those living northeast of Egypt, the Phillistines. They were more closely related to Greeks and actually had no ethnical, linguistic or historic relation or connection to Arabia.

Canaan first appeared in the 15th century B.C. and was referred to as "Eretz Bnei Visrael" or the "Land of the Children of Israel." During the Persian Period, the area that is now Israel and Syria was called Coele-Syria, during the 5th century B.C., Herodotus, a greek historian, used the word "Palaistine", referring to the coastal strip inhabited by Phillistine

Those living in what Roman Emperor Hadrian named Palestine, were known as Palestinians but this included Christians, Jews and Muslims as well as any people of any ethnic or religious affiliation. Basically, it was the term used to define anyone living in that territory.

It wasn't until Khalil Bayda who was a Palestinian scholar, educator, translator and novelist , used the term "Palestinian" to describe the Palestine Arabic speakers in 1898 did the concept of a Palestinian people begin. In June 1913, the media began to write of the concept of a Palestinian identity, compelling Ruhl al-Khalidi, an Ottoman paliamentarian and Muslim Jerusalemite to write the articl "The Palestinian Race' for the newspaper "Filastin" in which he argued that the Zionists were trying to make Palestine an exclusionary society.

After the fall of the Ottoman Empire with the British conquest of the country in WW1 in which Britain took control of the area, Palestine became a separate entity. A mandate held by the British empire and approved by the league of nations, the name "Palestine" was designated to that area, which included present day Israel and Jordan.

Bernard Lewis, an influential scholar of Islam and a Middle East historian, who was known for his research on the history, culture and politics of the islamic world, said the Jews in that region rejected the name "Palestine" because they associated that name with the mostly successful attempt by the Romans to destroy the Jewish culture in Israel. He also found that Arabs at that time, saw the name "Palestine" as a British imperialist collusion with Zionists to take a part of the Arab homeland, they felt no attachment to "palestine" as they believed it should remain a part of southern Syria.

In 1920, the French defeated Syria and disposed King Faisal and Musa Kazim al-Husayni, a Palestinian leader, stated "after the recent events in Damascus, we have to effect a complete change in our plans here. Southern Syria no longer exists. We must defend Palestine."

The Third Palestinian Congress, also called the Third Arab Palestinian Congress, was founded in 1921. It was attended by 36 delegates and held in the wake of the San Remo Conference which gave Britain a mandate over Palestine and appointed Herbert Samuel as the High commissioner.

The delegates were against this appointment, protesting these decisions while appealing to the Muslims in India as well as the Pope, bringing the eyes of the world to Palestine and the dangers to the Jews living there. Musa Kazim al Husayni headed a delegation to London whose purpose was to alter British policies and remained there until June 1922.

Palestine was proclaimed a state on November 15, 1988, when the Palestinian Liberation Council, which is the legislative body of the PLO, adopted the Palestinian Declaration of Independence, but that declaration was not recognized as legitimate by the world's leaders at that time. November 29, 2012 the United Nations General Assembly finally recognized Palestine as a "non member observer state", voting 138 in favor, 9 against and 41 absent. Since then, they have been recognized by over 135 countries but the international community still are divided on the status of Palestine, with some countries still considering it to be a sovereign state.

On May 14, 1948, Jewish Agency Chairman, David Ben-Gurion, proclaimed the State of Israel, establishing the first Jewish state in over 2000 years. President Harry S Truman recognized the State of Israel on the same day, along with Russia and many other world wide governments.

Immediately following the proclamation, 5 Arab states, Egypt, Iraq, Lebanon, Syria and Transjordan (Jordan today) invaded Israel. Although Israel was short on weapons and training, their morale was high from just defeating al-Husseini's army and combined with internal problems within the Arab armies as well as a secret relation between King Abdullah of Jordan, who opposed a Palestine state and Israel led to a small army of Israeli forces defeating the invaders.

Has there always been fighting between the Arabs and Jews? Ancient Israelites, who were descended from the Hebrews, lived in the land of Canaan starting around 1200 BC. The Arabs, who are actually descendants from the Ishmaelites, began immigrating to the area around 7th century BC, that is when the war between the Arabs and Israelites began.

The Crusades were launched on November 27, 1095 by Pope Urban II to liberate Jerusalem from Islamic control. Jews and christians were not allowed to build new temples, worship at their temples and had a choice of either converting to Islam or to stay alive, pay a monthly tax called a "jizzya." The crusades were launched because of religious persecution at the hands of the Muslims, the Pope didn't send out his army because he felt like beheading people one day but to give Christians and Jews access to Jerusalem, the holiest city to Jews and Christians alike.

But is that when the conflict that has lasted for almost 2000 years started? The conflict between Christians, Jews and Arabs I believe began with

Muhammed during the 7th century. Before Islam, the Arabian Pennisula was a very diverse home to many different religions, Polytheism, monotheism, Christianity and Judaism as well as Zoroastrianism. The people were free to worship whatever religion or deity they wanted to, A shrine in Mecca housed statues of all the different gods and godesses worshipped at that time, the Kabba as it was called, is believed to of housed atleast 360 different statues. Today, what it holds inside is unknown to the world as anyone who is not a Muslim is not allowed to enter the cities of Mecca or Medina.

According to a study by the Anti-defamation League published on their website on September 9, 2020, they conducted a "Global 100" survey of the acceptance of antisemitic beliefs in 100 countries around the world in 2014, 2015, 2017 and 2019. They state that there was a high rate of antisemitic beliefs in Muslim majority countries such as the Middle East and North Africa as we;; as Muslim respondents living in Western Europe .

The question they asked was did the responder have negative feelings towards Jews?

Saudi Arabia 74%

Iraq 92%

West Bank and Gaza 93%

Average score for Muslim majority countries is 74%, 74% of Muslim majority countries hold negative opinions or feeling for Jews, Gaza with a whopping 93% acceptance of antisemitic beliefs. Where is this hatred coming from? Hate is a learned emotion, no child is born with that emotion already part of their psyche. This hatred for the Jewish people and Israel is a problem that will not go away until the root of the problem is treated.

Textbooks in the Middle Eastern schools teach children to hate Jews and Christians. European policymakers found the violence and antisemitism in for example, Palestinian textbooks, to have been a part of the education system there for years. They passed legislation in 2018, 2020 and 2021 that did nothing more than condemn the textbooks, but the Palestinian Authority ignored them. A study by the George Eckert Institute on Palestine's textbooks confirmed that Palestine hasn't made any effort to change its textbooks. They also found that Palestine textbooks included values of human rights but their textbooks do not apply human rights to Israel or Jews.

The council on Foreign Relations published a study on Palestinian textbooks and their findings were even more disturbing. The paper, "PALESTINIAN ELEMENTARY SCHOOL CURRICULUM 2016-2017:RADICALIZATION AND REVIVAL OF THE PLO PROGRAM"
The new Palestinian curriculum which includes new textbooks for grades 1-4, the council discovered that the current curriculum teaches the students to be martyr's, it demonizes and denies the existence of Israel, denies the Holocaust ever happened, teaching instead that the number of Jews who died at the hands of the Nazi's was very small and they weren't killed by the Nazi's but instead died from starvation and disease.

The main focus of these new textbooks is the elimination of Israel "from the river to the sea."

Grade 3 textbook "OUR BEAUTIFUL LANGUAGE" VOL 2 2016-2017 PAGE 64 reads:

"I vow I shall sacrifice my blood, to saturate the land of the genrous and will eliminate the usurper from my country and will annihilate the remnants of the foreigners. Oh the land of Al-Aqsa and the Haram, on cradle of chivalry and generosity, Patient, be patient as victory is ours, dawn is emerging from the oppression."

The full study can be found here: https://www.impact-se.org/wp-content/uploads/PA-Curriculum-2017-Revised.pdf

Regardless of what you may believe, if you're one of these idiots out protesting in support of Palestine, you are also protesting in support of Hamas, Propaganda is a deadly effective tool that is used more today than at any other time in history, those who push propaganda as truth are one of the lowest life forms on earth because they will do anything to get what they are after and that includes defiling the dead. How pathetic and low can someone be that will lie about babies being butchered and beheaded?

Imran Ahmed, CEO of the center for Countering Digital Hate, a nonprofit organization that tracks disinformation from the Israeli/gaza war stated that the propagandists who have created so many AI created images coming out of Gaza that "show bodies of babies" are very skilled at targeting peoples deepest emotions.

Jean-Claude Goldenstein, CEO of CREOpoint, a tech company based in San Francisco and Paris that uses AI to test the validity of online pictures and videos and have created a database of the most viral "deepfakes" to have emerged from Gaza.

The possibility of much of what we are seeing coming out of Gaza and Palestine is very high, what better way to gain world wide sympathy than to create images that hit us deep in our gut, make us angry at the injustices being perpetrated so we rise up against Israel, their sworn enemy. I am sure some, no a lot of people will be saying that this is just some crazy conspiracy theory, but what if it isn't?

This will be a condensed version as I will be talking about this a little later in the book but here is a quick history lesson for you.

After the fall of the Ottaman Empire, Hassan al-Banna wanted Islam to go back to it's roots and ways- so he and 6 other people founded the Muslim Brotherhood in 1928 and that organization is the largest Muslim organization in the world, having atleast 2000 sister branches all over the world, one being Hamas. Banna had a deep admiration for someone during WW2 that no one ever seems to talk about and that person was none other than Adolf Hitler.

Banna had Mein Kamp translated into Arabic and even went to Germany, spending time learning from Hitler and also helped to recruit Arabs to their cause. There were plans made by Banna to bring gas chambers and camps like Aushwitz to the Middle East. Banna idolized Hitler, agreed with his treatment of Jews, but he also learned how important propaganda is when fighting a war.

The Nazi's came into power in 1933, the constitution in Germany at that time guaranteed freedom of speech and freedom of the press. Through subtle decrees, the Nazi's slowly abolished these civil rights, thereby destroying democracy in Germany. In 1934, it became illegal to criticize or say anything deragatory about Adold Hitler or the Nazi government (sound familiar) and how they did this is through censorship.
    1.) they closed down or took over any anti-nazi newspapers ensuring
        they controlled what news appeared in the paper
    2.) they also applied the same tactic to radio and news reels. The
        only information German citizens received was what the Hitler
        wanted them to see. It's easier to mold someone's mind or
        way of thinking if you control what information they get.

     3.) They banned or burned books that were catagorized as

          un-German.

     4.) They even went so far as controlling what the German soldiers

          wrote home to their loved ones during the war.

     Censorship isn't the only propaganda tactic that Hitler and the Nazi's used. In March 1933, Joseph Goebbels led a new ministry called the "Reich Ministry of Enlightenment and Propaganda." They centralized their efforts in this new ministry, controlling every aspect of information or false information being fed to the German population. Some examples are:

     1.) Glorifying Adolf Hitler, using his image on every postcard, poster

          and in every newspaper and newsreel. They were made to

          believe he was their champion or savior so to speak.

     2.) They spread false, negative images about Jews the same

          way they did with lies about Hitler. Jews were made out

          to be the cause of all bad things, demonized in magazines,

          films, media and even cartoons. Children were taught that

          Jews were born with tails, that they ate children and a

          thousand other lies, instilling a hatred and fear within them.

3.) They made radios cheaper and more affordable so that more
            German citizens would be able to listen to radio talk shows
            perpetuating Nazi ideas, news and beliefs. They broadcast
            Nazi speeches and celebratory Nazi Party rallies, further
            indoctrinating German citizens.
4.) Created youth groups like the Hitler Youth and League of
            German Girls, further fostering Nazi mentality.

During periods that proceeded legislation or executive measures against Jews, Gobbel would flood all media outlets with propaganda, reminding the German citizens they were fighting a was against foreign enemies, and that the Jews were helping Germans enemies subvertly, creating a society that accepted and welcomed violence against Jews, especially in 1935 and in 1938.

They also used propaganda to slowly brainwash German citizens into accepting the impending measures they intended to use against the Jews, they did this by making it appear they were stepping in and regaining control and restoring order from the chaos the Jews had caused.

In Eastern Europe and gained territories like Czechoslovakia and Poland, they employed real and fabricated discrimination propaganda against ethnic

Germans living in those areas. After the German invasion into Russia, they used propaganda to citizens at home, soldiers, police officers and all non german auxillaries that were serving in any occupied territory to make them all believe that Soviet Communism went hand in hand with European Jewry. The presented Hitler and the Nazi government as the defender of "Western" culture against the "Judeo-Bolshevik Threat." They used fear to control the masses by painting an apocolyptical picture of what would happen if Germany lost, if the German citizens did not support Hitler and the Nazi's in their conquest.

Movies portrayed Jews as "subhuman," "cultural parasites consumed by money and sex. Newspapers printed cartoons using antisemitic characters in very negative ways to depict Jews. They convinced German citizens that Jews were enemies, the most dangerous of all enemies of the German Reich and must be permanently removed.

When they implemented the "Final Solution," (mass murder of jews in concetration camps) the SS officials at the camps forced the Jews to send out postcards that said they were being treated well and living conditions were great. This was used as a means to ensure that the operation ran smoothly, if other Jews believed that it was a good place they were being taken, they wouldn't fight them or run away, they would come happily to their death.

How Hitler managed to make an entire country support and fight for him is through propaganda and

control. He controlled any and all news they received, they had no idea that what they read in the newspapers or heard on the radio was all a very elaborate, well thought out and executed plan.
This method of waging war is still being used today but on an even larger scale thanks to social media and the internet.

Terrorist groups like Hamas and Hezbollah learned from history the effectiveness of a propaganda campaign, using video, pictures, news clips, Instagram,. Facebook. X(twitter) and more to recruit and push their narrative. Hamas has been banned from facebook and instagram, but their message is still being heard on those social media sites because accounts that sympathize with these terrorists have seen the number of followers go from a few hundred to hundred of thousands. Within 24 hours after the October 7, 2023 attack, Researchers for Strategic Dialogue, they track hate and extremeism online found that multiple posts supporting October 7 terrorist actions got over 16 million views. Telegram, a "encrypted messaging" app still allows Hamas and even hosts an official account of Al-Qassam Brigades (Hamas's military wing)

Allegations have arisen that the UNRWA (United Nations Relief and Works Agency) employed over 450 operatives from Hamas and other armed militant groups in Palestine. The religion that is the majority within the UNRWA is not surprising, Muslims make up almost 80% of the UNRWA employees with more than 10% having ties to Hamas and other terrorist organizations. A network of Hamas tunnels were found under the UNRWA's headquarters in Gaza which housed a very sophisticated data center with electricity cables running directly up from the tunnels into the headquarter building connecting directly to the UNRWA's electricity network. Just two weeks earlier, intelligence reports confirmed that atleast 12 UNRWA members participated in the October 7th attack. That 10% of UNRWA employess that have ties to Hamas represents a whopping 1200 persons currently employed by UNRWA that are Hamas or Palestinian Islamic Jihad operatives.

A ten year long research concluded that UNRWA staff frequently and continually incite antisemitism and promote terrorism against Israel on social media platforms and UNRWA in Gaza has been fully infiltrated by Hamas and therefore is no longer capable of providing neutral humanitarian aide in the region.

within a UNRWA school located Nuseirat, Central Gaza, the IDF found and identified a Hamas war room and from documents discovered in Gaza, confirmed atleast 500 UNRWA employees in Gaza serve in mil;itary positions within Hamas. So you must ask yourself this question-if UNRWA, part of the United Nations, if they truly have been infiltrated and compromised, is the information the United Nations if providing us accurate or false??? How can you trust what they are telling us if the perpetrators of October 7th are those who are giving us information? The fox who is in the hen house eating your chickens is the one providing you information on how many chickens he is eating-would you trust that? You would not only be a fool but you'd be a complete idiot to accept everything the United Nations and Palestine have been telling the rest of the world without questioning the motives.

Back to how long have Palestinians been Palestinians? The claim that they are descendents from Phillistines is not only inaccurate but a complete lie. Phillistines settled in the southern part of Canaan, now Israel and Gaza and were also called the Sea People. The story of David and Goliath is just one story of the conflict between Jews and Phillistines. They worshipped many different Gods, the main God being "Dagon." In the new testament, Phillistine is often used to summarize those who oppose moral or spiritual progress.

Contrary to what some may think, Phillistines were actually Greek and are ethnically related to the Egyptians which through dna testing of mummies, it has been proven that Egyptians were not Arabic. Phillistine pottery that has been discovered, resembles Homeric Greek civilizations, the materials used providing an undeniable connection. In the same areas, archeoligists found early Greek weapons, armor, dress and similar burial methods. If the Phillistines were Greek and not Arabic, what is the basis for the claim that Palestinians are Phillistines?

The Roman Emperor Hadrian defeated the Jews in the Bar Kochba rebellion was the result of many years of conflict between Jews and the Romans. The Romans won the war by adopting a "scorched earth" strategy that laid waste to the rebels and country side.

The majority of the Jewish population was either killed, exiled or enslaved but coins that have been discovered show that for a brief period, there was an independent Jewish state that existed.

The after math of the war was more horrific than the actual war itself, Emperor Hadrian permanently changing the name of Judea to Palestina, effectively erasing its Jewish past. All Jewish rituals and laws were banned and most Jewish religious leaders were martyred and Jerusalem, the birth place of Jesus, was permanently converted into a pagan city called Aelia Capitolina. All Jews were forbidden from living within site, shifting the demography to that of non-jewish people and thus it remained for almost 2,000 years.

Very few Jewish communities remained and Jews would be state less until 1948 when Israel was given back to the Jewish population. Regardless if you are pro-Palestinian or pro-Israel, historical, undisputable facts prove beyond question, that Jews lived in the land now known as Israel for hundreds of years before Palestinians laid their unrightful claim.

When watching tv or a video, reading an article, when doing anything where you are being fed any type of information, don't let yourself fall victim to propaganda, but propaganda isn't always what we've been led to believe which in itself is propaganda. We've been brainwashed to hate leaders like Putin and idolize leaders like Zelensky but is what we've been convinced to believe true and accurate? Or is it part of a big lie to twist our way of thinking so that we fall into line with the agenda of those in power?

Remember Hitler and the fact that propaganda is the greatest tool he had, without his propaganda campaign he would not of made it as far as he did. Look beyond youtube and google, two of the most biased sites in existence if not the most. Just because news outlets like MSNBC and CNN post articles claiming something does not make those claims true, in fact, with most of main stream media, there are more lies and fabrications than truth. Closing your mind off to something because it's "conservative" does nothing but prove your stupidity and shallowness, because it's conservative does not make it wrong nor does it make it right but being a liberal doesn't mean you have all the answers on how people are supposed to live their lives.

Propaganda is just another name for a lie that is used by corrupt politicians, terrorist organizations, main stream media, social media, influencers, even teachers and professors, news groups, journalists- anyone who has a hidden agenda or ulterior motive that needs you to believe their lies in order to attain their goal. Look beyond the box you live in, knowledge is power so educate yourself. Recognize hypocracy and do something about it when you do find it, stand up for what's right but do it without violence, and once again EDUCATE YOURSELF so when you do stand up, you know without doubt you're standing for the right cause.